CW01602960

TIME SHIP

A Play by Alan Dapré

Illustrations by Mike Perkins

Series Editors: Steve Barlow and Steve Skidmore

Heinemann

Published by Heinemann Educational Publishers
Halley Court, Jordan Hill, Oxford OX2 8EJ
A division of Reed Educational and Professional Publishing Ltd

OXFORD MELBOURNE AUCKLAND
JOHANNESBURG BLANTYRE GABORONE
IBADAN PORTSMOUTH NH (USA) CHICAGO

© Alan Dapré, 2000
Original illustrations © Heinemann Educational Publishers 2000

All rights reserved. No part of this publication may be reproduced in any material form (including photocopying or storing it in any medium by electronic means and whether or not transiently or incidentally to some other use of this publication) without the prior written permission of the copyright owner, except in accordance with the provisions of the Copyright, Designs and Patents Act 1988 or under the terms of a licence issued by the Copyright Licensing Agency Ltd, 90 Tottenham Court Road, London W1P 9HE. Applications for the copyright owner's written permission to reproduce any part of this publication should be addressed in the first instance to the publisher.

First published 2000
2004 2003 2002 2001 2000
10 9 8 7 6 5 4 3 2 1
ISBN 0 435 21392 X

Illustrations by Mike Perkins
Cover Design by Shireen Nathoo Design
Cover artwork by Paul Young
Designed by Artistix, Thame, Oxon
Printed and bound in Great Britain by Biddles Ltd

Tel: 01865 888058 www.heinemann.co.uk

Contents

Characters

BERG is leader of the space patrol. He has a secret.

PERI is second in command.

ZARA is the Science Officer of the space patrol.

HUGH is the computer on the spaceship 'Pandora'. He is a hologram.

SCENE ONE

The control deck of the spaceship 'Pandora'

Peri enters and checks the room.

PERI: All clear.

(She sits as Berg enters.)

BERG: You're sitting in the Captain's chair.

PERI: I see no Captain. Just the ship he left behind.

BERG: Stand up. That's an order.

(She stands slowly.)

PERI: As you wish.

(Zara enters.)

ZARA: Look at this, they even left their food.

(She picks up three green pills.)

PERI: I don't blame them.

ZARA: It's odd. Why would a Captain and his crew want to jump ship?

BERG: That's what you're here to find out.

ZARA: My scanners show no one is on board. The ship is simply drifting in space.

BERG: No life forms at all?

ZARA: Just the three of us.

PERI: I bet there never was any life in this tin can. Maybe the crew left because they were fed up.

ZARA: Being in space is dull.

PERI: They don't tell you that at Training Camp. I wanted to explore new worlds. Not old spaceships.

BERG: What do you know about this spaceship, Peri?

PERI: It's a Z Class Cargo ship. Very basic. It must be two hundred years old.

ZARA: And the rest. This computer should be in a museum.

(Peri taps a key on the computer.)

PERI: It has no power. See? The screen is dead.

ZARA: My scanners show that the ship is very low on power. What is left is being sent to the engines.

BERG: *(Firmly)* I want this computer working, Zara. It may give us some clues about what has happened here. Can you do it?

ZARA: Yes, I'll get the power we need from our ship.

BERG: What are you waiting for?

(Zara exits.)

PERI: Berg, what do you make of all this?

BERG: I don't. I need more facts. One wrong move could cost a life. Maybe yours.

PERI: I can look after myself.

BERG: Is the ship safe?

PERI: *(Looking at her scanner)* There are no traps.

BERG: Good.

PERI: I am good.

BERG: I know. You could go far. As long as you obey my orders.

PERI: Sure, Patrol Leader.

(Enter Zara.)

BERG: *(To Zara)* How long will you need to set up a power link?

ZARA: I just need to join this lead to the computer. There, it's done.

BERG: Switch it on!

(She switches on the computer.)

I want to know everything about this ship. Its crew, its mission, its cargo. Open the ship's log. It may tell us what happened here.

ZARA: Log open, sir.

BERG: It's blank.

PERI: The data has been erased.

BERG: *(Angrily)* It seems that someone didn't want us to read it.

ZARA: Maybe the Captain had something to hide?

BERG: Maybe. I want a plan of this ship.

ZARA: The plan data has been erased too. Everything has been wiped off.

(To Berg) This is a waste of time. Let's go back.

BERG: No, Zara. We have a job to do.

PERI: I don't like this, Berg. A ship with no crew, just drifting in space.

BERG: I give the orders. We stay.

(To Zara.)

You're meant to be good with computers! *Do* something.

PERI: This always works.

(Peri kicks the base of the computer. It hums.)

ZARA: *(Amazed)* You've started up a program.

PERI: Told you it works.

(Enter Hugh.)

HUGH: Greetings.

PERI: Don't move. I'm armed.

HUGH: *(Sighing)* Your laser cannot harm me. Put it away.

BERG: *(To Zara)* You said that no one else was on this ship. Only us. Wrong again.

ZARA: My scanner isn't picking up any signs of life.

HUGH: You are correct.

PERI: It looks human.

HUGH: I am not alive.

BERG: What are you?

HUGH: I am the ship's computer.

PERI: Amazing.

HUGH: I am a hologram in the shape of a human.

ZARA: I get it. Hugh is short for "human hologram".

HUGH: That is correct. The Captain chose my name. He thought it made me more – human.

BERG: Greetings, Hugh. Peri, stand down.

(Peri puts her laser away.)

HUGH: Who booted up my holo-file?

PERI: Boot is the right word!

HUGH: I shut myself down after the Captain and his crew left.

BERG: Z Class cargo ships do not have holograms.

HUGH: This one does.

ZARA: There are a lot of high tech machines on board. I would not expect to see them on a cargo ship.

BERG: I see. But nothing here is what it seems. Is it, Hugh?

HUGH: What do you mean?

BERG: You know what's on this ship. You know what we're here for.

(Hugh smiles at Berg.)

HUGH: Yes. I do. *(Berg, Zara and Peri sway as the ship makes a sharp turn. Hugh does not move.)*

PERI: Who's driving this thing?

ZARA: What's happening?

HUGH: I have just switched on the auto-pilot.

ZARA: Where are you taking us?

(Peri looks out of a window.)

PERI: I don't need a computer to tell me where this ship is heading. Towards that sun!

BERG: *(To Hugh)* Turn this ship around!

HUGH: *(Coldly)* I'm sorry, I can't.

ZARA: If we get too close to that sun, the ship will never get away.

PERI: We'll be dragged into it and burnt up.

BERG: Zara, I need you to turn the ship around and get us away from that sun. Now!

ZARA: I can't. The auto-pilot is steering the ship.

BERG: *(Angry)* Then over ride it.

ZARA: *(Worried)* I don't have the over ride code.

HUGH: You have to leave this ship. Your lives will be in danger if you stay.

BERG: *(Angry)* Computer! Over ride the auto-pilot.

HUGH: I can't do that. You will have to leave.

PERI: It's no help at all!

BERG: We must stay calm, Peri. Hugh wants to destroy this ship.

HUGH: You are correct. Nothing you say, will change my mind.

ZARA: *(To Hugh)* How long before we go into the Sun?

HUGH: This ship will be destroyed in sixteen earth minutes. You will die unless you leave.

BERG: No! I'm going to stay until I get what I came for. We are all going to stay!

(Blackout.)

Scene Two

On the spaceship 'Pandora': corridor outside Laboratory A.

PERI: This is the main lab.

BERG: Tell me how to get past that door.

HUGH: I cannot let you access that data.

BERG: You know what is in there, don't you Hugh?

HUGH: I am the ship's computer. It is my job to know.

BERG: Then answer me this. Did the Captain and crew take it?

HUGH: It?

BERG: Don't play games. You know what I mean. There is something behind that door. Did it kill the crew?

HUGH: No. It did not.

PERI: *(Angry)* Open this door, creep!

HUGH: I sense your tone is one of anger.

BERG: We would all feel much happier if you let us into the lab.

HUGH: That is not possible.

BERG: I knew this would happen. Zara, pick the lock.

(Zara tries to pick the lock on the door.)

ZARA: Why is there a lab on board? I thought this was a cargo ship.

BERG: Because it's a secret lab.

PERI: No one looks twice at a cargo ship.

BERG: The crew on board were making something.

ZARA: So what is this big secret?

BERG: Why don't you tell her what "it" is, Hugh?

HUGH: It is clear to me that you know the secret of this ship.

ZARA: *I* don't! What are we talking about?

HUGH: The Time Box.

ZARA: What do you mean? What is this Time Box?

HUGH: It is a machine that lets humans travel in time. It has taken many years to make.

ZARA: How long?

HUGH: Two hundred years.

BERG: This ship was a science ship. The crew must have built the Time Box.

HUGH: That is right.

ZARA: But why not build the lab on a planet?

HUGH: A cargo ship can travel anywhere. It would be bad to stay in one place. Someone would try to steal the secret of time travel.

PERI: It would be worth a lot.

BERG: Time travel has always been a dream. On this ship, that dream came true.

HUGH: Yes. You know the secret.

BERG: Here's something I don't know. How does the Time Box work?

HUGH: The Time Box has never been fully tested.

BERG: Then it may not work?

HUGH: The early model could send very small objects backwards and forwards in time.

BERG: *(Quietly so only Hugh can hear)* I was told by the scientists who were on board this heap that they had made it work.

HUGH: *(Softly)* I cannot confirm your data.

BERG: *(Quietly)* They said the Time Box could send the whole ship back in time, and everybody on it.

HUGH: *(Coldly)* I cannot confirm your data.

PERI: Hurry, Zara.

BERG: Pick the lock!

ZARA: How big is this Time Box anyway?

BERG: Don't talk, just *do*.

(Zara bangs the door.)

ZARA: *(Upset)* I can't unlock it. We must leave now.

BERG: No! You stay until I – we – get the Time Box.

ZARA: I'm leaving.

BERG: I said no!

(He aims a laser at Zara.)

The Time Box is behind that door. It wasn't on the crew's escape pod.

ZARA: What escape pod?

BERG: The one we took apart bit by bit.

PERI: We found nothing.

ZARA: We?

PERI: Yes. We.

ZARA: Not you too, Peri. You're both mad.

PERI: I don't think so.

BERG: It isn't madness. That tiny box could buy me my own planet.

ZARA: Who would pay that much?

BERG: That would be saying.

PERI: Don't forget my part in this, Berg. It was rather messy taking over that escape pod.

BERG: I'll pay you your share.

ZARA: This was meant to be a simple job to find out what happened to this ship.

BERG: Once upon a time! *(Coldly)* You're only here to get us into that room. So do it!

PERI: Hugh, how long until the ship is pulled in by the Sun?

HUGH: Eight minutes.

ZARA: We're in!

(Zara and Peri run through the door, into the lab.)

BERG: Now we're alone, I want to ask you something.

HUGH: Go ahead.

BERG: Why did the Captain and his Crew leave?

HUGH: I shut down the life support system. They had to leave. I made sure they had to go.

BERG: Why?

HUGH: So the Time Box could not be used against other human beings. It is dangerous.

BERG: How do you know that? You're just a hologram – a computer.

HUGH: I have studied what humans would do with time travel. Five hundred years ago they discovered nuclear power. They could have used it to help the world. But humans used it to make bombs.

BERG: That was a long time ago.

HUGH: People lived in fear. Think of the dangers if the Time Box falls into the wrong hands.

BERG: If!

(Peri and Zara return, carrying the Time Box.)

PERI: Is this what you're after, Patrol Leader Berg?

BERG: Yes. Well done. Now pass it over to me.

PERI: No. There's been a change of plan. I'm going to leave now, and take this with me.

BERG: Stop! Or –

PERI: Or you'll blast a nice big hole in this box? Not a good idea.

BERG: Maybe we can do a deal.

PERI: No deals. Get back onto the bridge.

Scene Three

On the command bridge, by the airlock. Peri stands near Berg and Zara. Hugh is nearby.

BERG: Now that you have the Time Box what do you plan to do with it?

PERI: Sell it.

BERG: Join me. Together, we could have a great future. Or a great past!

PERI: No. You're history, Berg.

(The ship shakes. All except Hugh stumble.)

ZARA: The Pandora can't take much more. We must get back onto our ship now.

PERI: I go alone. You're all staying here.

ZARA: You can't leave us. Let's open the airlock door and all go.

PERI: You are going nowhere.

(The ship shakes. Berg leaps forward as Peri falls. Berg grabs the Time Box.)

BERG: All good things come to those who wait. I've got what I came for. I do like a happy ending. It's a pity you won't be sharing it with me.

PERI: *(Begging)* Take me with you.

BERG: You're no use to me now, Peri. I can't trust you.

ZARA: Berg, the Sun's grip on this ship is growing by the second. We must go soon, or our ship will be trapped too.

BERG: What's all this about "we?"

PERI: Don't be stupid, Zara. He's going to leave us both behind.

ZARA: When HQ hears about this they will find you.

BERG: HQ won't hear about it. You won't be around to tell them. Nor will I. You see, Patrol Leader Berg will soon be no more. I am about to start a new life under a new name.

PERI: While we end ours here.

BERG: It's time for me to say goodbye.

PERI: Why not stay and join in the fun?

BERG: You know what they say – if you can't stand the heat, get out of the spaceship.

ZARA: Hugh, you must stop him.

(Berg enters the airlock.)

HUGH: I cannot hold him back. I have no body. I am made from light.

ZARA: You're made from light. That's it!
Don't you see? Blind him with it!

HUGH: Blind him?

ZARA: Yes! Turn your power up as high as it will go.

(Berg turns to look back. Zara covers her eyes and looks away. There is a blinding flash.)

BERG: My eyes!

PERI: I can't see!

ZARA: Give me the Time Box.

(Zara grabs the Time Box from Berg. Blinded, Berg crashes round the bridge with his arms in front of him, trying to catch Zara.)

BERG: Give it back! It's mine.

HUGH: *(To Zara)* You must not let any humans use the Time Box. It is too dangerous.

BERG: That box is worth a fortune! Give it to me!

HUGH: The Time Box has the power to loop Time – the same way a computer can loop a sample of music so it is played over and over again.

BERG: Give me that box!

HUGH: It could play the same things – the same events – over and over again.

BERG: Light – my eyes are clearing. I can see again!

(To Zara)

Now give – it – to – me. It's mine!

ZARA: It's nobody's! Hugh is right. The Time Box must never be used!

(The ship shakes. An alarm rings.)

HUGH: Your time is up, Berg. Both ships are trapped. Now there can be no escape.

PERI: For any of us.

BERG: My life is not over yet.

(Laughing, he grabs the Time Box from Zara.)

A stitch in Time saves mine.
Maybe yours.

ZARA: There's no way out, Berg. Your greed has trapped us here.

BERG: You're wrong. There is one way.

PERI: The Time Box.

BERG: Now we all have nothing to lose.

(He opens the Time Box.)

PERI: You don't know what you're doing.

BERG: Time will tell.

HUGH: No, don't do it you fool!

(Berg presses a button in the Time Box.)

BERG: It's time!

(Blackout.)

Scene Four

The lights fade up to reveal the control deck of the spaceship 'Pandora'. Peri enters and checks the room.

PERI: All clear.

(She sits as Berg enters.)

BERG: You're sitting in the Captain's chair.

PERI: I see no Captain. Just the ship he left behind.

BERG: Stand up. That's an order.

(She stands slowly.)

PERI: As you wish.

(Zara enters as the lights begin to fade.)

ZARA: Look at this, they even left their food.

(She picks up three green pills.)

PERI: I don't blame them.

ZARA: It's odd. Why would a Captain and his crew want to jump ship?

BERG: That's what you're here to find out.

(Blackout.)